Travel America's Landmarks

Exploring the Gateway Arch

by Emma Huddleston

FOCUS READERS

BEACON

www.focusreaders.com

Focus Readers is distributed by North Star Editions:
sales@northstareditions.com | 888-417-0195

Produced for Focus Readers by Red Line Editorial.

Photographs ©: f11photo/iStockphoto, cover, 1; stevegeer/iStockphoto, 4, 14, 29; RudyBalasko/ Shutterstock Images, 7; Oscar White/Corbis Historical/VCG/Getty Images, 8; Fred Waters/AP Images, 11, 13; North Wind Picture Archives, 17; RudyBalasko/iStockphoto, 19; Davel5957/iStockphoto, 20–21; inkit/iStockphoto, 22; traveler1116/iStockphoto, 25; Red Line Editorial, 27

Library of Congress Cataloging-in-Publication Data
Names: Huddleston, Emma, author.
Title: Exploring the Gateway Arch / by Emma Huddleston.
Description: Lake Elmo, MN : Focus Readers, [2020] | Series: Travel America's
  landmarks | Includes bibliographical references and index. | Audience:
  Grades 4-6.
Identifiers: LCCN 2019006355 (print) | LCCN 2019007305 (ebook) | ISBN
  9781641859882 (pdf) | ISBN 9781641859240 (ebook) | ISBN 9781641857864
  (hardcover) | ISBN 9781641858557 (pbk.)
Subjects: LCSH: Gateway Arch (Saint Louis, Mo.)--Juvenile literature. | Saint
  Louis (Mo.)--Buildings, structures, etc.--Juvenile literature.
Classification: LCC F474.S265 (ebook) | LCC F474.S265 H83 2020 (print) | DDC
  977.8/66--dc23
LC record available at https://lccn.loc.gov/2019006355

Printed in the United States of America
Mankato, MN
May, 2019

About the Author

Emma Huddleston lives in the Twin Cities with her husband. She enjoys writing children's books, but she likes reading novels even more. When she is not writing or reading, she likes to stay active by running and swing dancing. She thinks America's landmarks are fascinating and wants to visit them all!

Chapter 1

Built to Remember

People tilt their heads back. They stare up toward the sky. They are looking at the Gateway Arch. The metal shines bright in the sunlight.

The Gateway Arch is the tallest **monument** in the United States.

 The Gateway Arch is the tallest arch in the world.

It stands 630 feet (192 m) tall. It is more than twice as tall as the Statue of Liberty.

The Gateway Arch is in St. Louis, Missouri. It stands in an open, grassy area. City buildings and busy roads surround it on one side. The Mississippi River rushes past on the other.

Fun Fact

Each leg of the Arch has 1,076 steps. But visitors take a **tram** to the top.

 The Gateway Arch is a recognizable part of the St. Louis skyline.

The Arch was built as a symbol of **freedom** and change. When people visit, they remember key moments in US history.

Chapter 2

A Winning Design

In the 1940s, the city of St. Louis wanted a monument to show the city's role in US history. St. Louis held a design competition in 1947. The winning **architect** planned to make a big wooden arch.

Eero Saarinen won the competition to design St. Louis's monument.

Buildings would fill the grassy area nearby. But these plans did not happen. The city needed more money for the project.

In 1957, money became available. The architect designed new plans. This time, he planned to make the arch out of metal. The grassy area would be open. A museum would be underground. Paths would lead to the historic Old Courthouse nearby.

Construction began in 1963. The Arch was tricky to build.

 Construction of the Gateway Arch lasted more than one year.

The measurements had to be just right. Metal pieces were made in Pennsylvania. Trains brought them to St. Louis.

Workers built the two legs of the Arch at the same time. The legs needed to meet in the middle. It would be a disaster if the pieces didn't fit. In 1965, workers put the final piece in place. The legs came together perfectly. St. Louis had its monument.

Fun Fact

The Arch and the surrounding land became the Gateway Arch National Park in 2018.

 Workers prepare to insert the final piece of the Gateway Arch.

Today, the park is a peaceful place in a busy city. Two ponds reflect sunlight. Trees line the sidewalks. People travel to see the Arch. They learn about the history of St. Louis.

Chapter 3

Many Symbols

The Gateway Arch has another name. The Arch is also called the Gateway to the West. An important journey to the West began near St. Louis. The Arch stands as a reminder of this exploration.

From the top of the Arch, people can see for miles.

President Thomas Jefferson bought a huge piece of land in 1803. It doubled the size of the United States. The land stretched from the Mississippi River to the Rocky Mountains.

Jefferson asked Meriwether Lewis and William Clark to explore the land. They led a group of more than 30 people. The explorers started their trip where the Mississippi and Missouri Rivers meet. They left by boat.

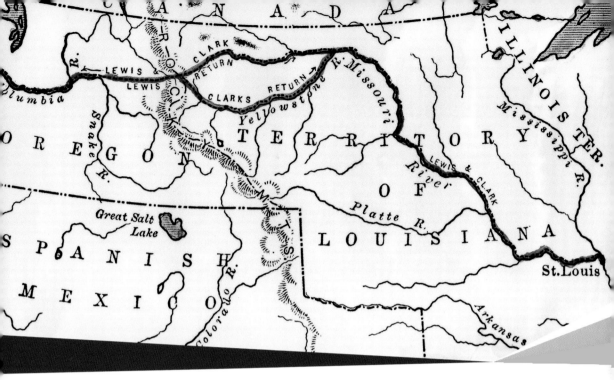

 Lewis and Clark started out near St. Louis on their journey to the West.

Lewis and Clark traveled from 1804 to 1806. They wrote about the animals and plants they saw. They met American Indians who were living in the West. They brought their findings back to Jefferson.

Lewis and Clark became famous for their exploration.

In addition to exploration, the Arch also stands for freedom and change. The two legs of the Arch frame the Old Courthouse. Together, the buildings represent how US laws have changed. People

Fun Fact

The Old Courthouse was originally a brick building completed in 1828. But the brick was replaced in the 1850s.

 The Arch architects included the Old Courthouse in their designs for St. Louis's monument.

have fought for their rights in the Old Courthouse. These people have helped shape US **culture** today.

The Old Courthouse

The Old Courthouse is famous for two historic **cases**. In the 1850s, Dred and Harriet Scott were enslaved. They fought for freedom in the Old Courthouse. Their case went to the Supreme Court. But the Court said enslaved people were property. This decision helped lead to the US Civil War (1861–1865).

In the 1870s, Virginia Minor fought for women's right to vote. She brought her case to the Old Courthouse. This case also went to the Supreme Court. Minor lost her case. But she helped **advance** women's rights.

The Old Courthouse is in walking distance of the Gateway Arch.

Chapter 4

Visiting the Gateway Arch

Visitors can go inside the Gateway Arch. Small trams take people to the top. Up to five people can go in one tram. At the top of the Arch, people look out through windows. They see the city of St. Louis.

Visitors head inside the museum beneath the Gateway Arch.

Visitors can also explore an underground museum. It has many **exhibits**. One teaches about how the Arch was built. One is about President Thomas Jefferson and exploring the West. Another exhibit teaches visitors about riverboats.

Fun Fact

Riverboats were important in St. Louis in the 1840s and 1850s. They brought food and supplies from other parts of the country.

> The Gateway Arch museum is underneath the Arch.

People can take riverboat tours. They see the Arch from the Mississippi River. Or they can take helicopter tours. They fly over the Arch and St. Louis.

Visitors can also walk around the park. Trees and open grounds make it feel separate from the busy city. People can walk to the Old Courthouse in less than 10 minutes. They can go on tours. They see what the building looked like in the 1800s.

Fun Fact

The Old Courthouse had 12 courtrooms at one point. Visitors can see two of the original courtrooms.

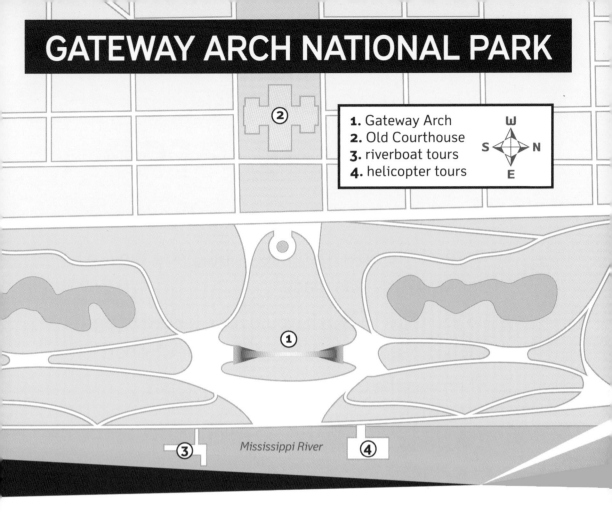

GATEWAY ARCH NATIONAL PARK

1. Gateway Arch
2. Old Courthouse
3. riverboat tours
4. helicopter tours

Mississippi River

The Arch stands for freedom, change, and exploration. Visitors remember US history. They learn that the United States is always changing and growing.

Gateway Arch

Write your answers on a separate piece of paper.

1. Write a letter to a friend describing how the Gateway Arch was made.

2. Do you think the Arch would have looked better if it had been made of wood? Why or why not?

3. When was the Gateway Arch completed?
   - **A.** 1965
   - **B.** 1804
   - **C.** 1947

4. Why is the Gateway Arch an important symbol of US history?
   - **A.** It is the tallest monument in the United States.
   - **B.** It represents important events in US history.
   - **C.** It was built along the Mississippi River.

5. What does **competition** mean in this book?

*St. Louis held a design **competition** in 1947. The winning architect planned to make a big wooden arch.*

    A. a plan for how to build something
    B. an event that many people try to win
    C. a large structure made of wood

6. What does **symbol** mean in this book?

*The Arch was built as a **symbol** of freedom and change. When people visit, they remember key moments in US history.*

    A. a place that many people visit
    B. an event that happened long ago
    C. a thing that stands for something else

Answer key on page 32.

Glossary

advance
To move forward or make progress.

architect
Someone who designs buildings and makes construction plans.

cases
Problems that people take to court so that a decision can
be made.

culture
The way a group of people live; their customs, beliefs, and laws.

exhibits
Public displays.

freedom
The right to think, speak, or do as one wants without being
stopped.

monument
A building or structure that is of historical interest or importance.

tram
A car that runs along tracks.

To Learn More

BOOKS

Davis, Hasan. *The Journey of York: The Unsung Hero of the Lewis and Clark Expedition*. North Mankato, MN: Capstone Editions, 2019.

Mattern, Joanne. *The Gateway Arch: Celebrating Western Expansion*. South Egremont, MA: Red Chair Press, 2018.

Mulhall, Jill K. *Lewis & Clark*. Huntington Beach, CA: Teacher Created Materials, 2017.

NOTE TO EDUCATORS

Visit **www.focusreaders.com** to find lesson plans, activities, links, and other resources related to this title.

Index

Answer Key: 1. Answers will vary; **2.** Answers will vary; **3.** A; **4.** B; **5.** B; **6.** C